Fish Babies

Catherine Veitch

Raintree

Raintree is an imprint of Capstone Global Library Limited, a company incorporated in England and Wales having its registered office at 7 Pilgrim Street, London, EC4V 6LB – Registered company number: 6695582

www.raintreepublishers.co.uk
myorders@raintreepublishers.co.uk

Text © Capstone Global Library Limited 2013
First published in hardback in 2013
Paperback edition first published in 2014
The moral rights of the proprietor have been asserted.

Edited by Daniel Nunn, Rebecca Rissman, and Catherine Veitch
Designed by Cynthia Della-Rovere
Picture research by Ruth Blair
Production by Victoria Fitzgerald
Originated by Capstone Global Library
Printed and bound in China

ISBN 978 1 406 25924 7 (hardback)
17 16 15 14 13
10 9 8 7 6 5 4 3 2 1

ISBN 978 1 406 25931 5 (paperback)
18 17 16 15 14
10 9 8 7 6 5 4 3 2 1

British Library Cataloguing in Publication Data
Veitch, Catherine.
Fish babies. -- (Animal babies)
597.1'392-dc23
A full catalogue record for this book is available from the British Library.

Acknowledgements
We would like to thank the following for permission to reproduce photographs: Naturepl pp. title page (© Nature Production), 6 (© Jane Burton), 7 (© David Fleetham), 8 (© Jurgen Freund), 9 (© Georgette Douwma), 10 (© Jane Burton), 11 (© Jane Burton), 12 (© Jane Burton), 13 (© David Fleetham), 14 (© Jane Burton), 16 (© Nature Production), 17 (© Mark Bowler), 19 (© Jane Burton), 20 (© Wild Wonders of Europe / Roggo), 22 (© Jane Burton, © Angelo Giampiccolo), 23 (© Jurgen Freund); Shutterstock pp. 4 (© Krzysztof Odziomek), 5 (© Cigdem Sean Cooper), 15 (© mnoor), 18 (© Dobermaraner), 21 (© Peter Leahy), 22 (© Kletr), 23 (© Kletr, © Cigdem Sean Cooper).

Front cover photograph of brown discus parent and babies reproduced with kind permission of Naturepl (© Nature Production).

We would like to thank Michael Bright for his invaluable help in the preparation of this book.

Every effort has been made to contact copyright holders of material reproduced in this book. Any omissions will be rectified in subsequent printings if notice is given to the publisher.

Contents

What is a fish?

Fish live in water.

gill

fin

Fish have gills. Fish have fins.

How are baby fish born?

egg

Most female fish lay eggs.

baby

egg

Sometimes fish babies hatch
from eggs.

larva inside an egg

Sometimes larvae hatch from eggs.

Larvae grow into baby fish.

babies inside

Some female fish do not lay eggs.

baby

They give birth to baby fish.

Where do fish lay their eggs?

Female fish lay their eggs in the water.

Some fish carry their eggs in their mouths.

nest made from plants

Some fish make nests for their eggs.

bubbles

This nest is made of bubbles.

Caring for baby fish

babies

Some fish care for their babies.

baby

This fish carries its babies in its mouth.

Some fish eat their own babies.

18

The baby fish hide to stay safe.

Growing up

Most baby fish look after
themselves. They feed on insects
and plants.

They hide from predators.

Life cycle of a fish

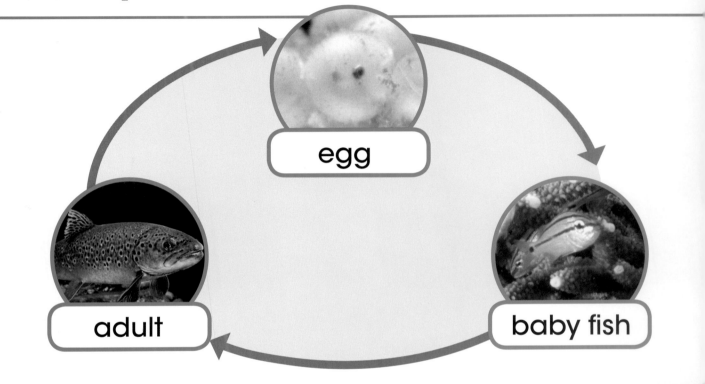

egg

adult

baby fish

A life cycle shows the different stages of an animal's life. This is the life cycle of a fish.

Picture glossary

 **fin** part of a fish that helps it to swim

 **gill** part of a fish that helps it to breathe

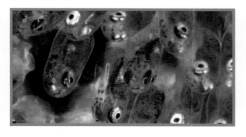 **larva** stage some fish have when they first hatch. More than one is larvae.

 **predator** animal that eats other animals

Index

Notes for parents and teachers

Before reading
Show children a collection of photos and videos of fish. National Geographic and BBC Nature are useful websites. Explain what a fish is and discuss the characteristics of fish.

After reading
- Mount photos of adult and baby fish on card, and play games of snap and pairs where the children have to match a baby fish with its parent. Model the correct pairs first.
- Ask children to label the parts of a fish: for example, fin, gill, tail, scales.
- Look at page 22 and discuss the life cycle stages of a fish. Mount photos of the egg, baby and adult stages and ask children to put the photos in order. Encourage children to draw a life cycle of a human to compare. Compare how different fish care for their babies. Discuss the care human babies need.
- To extend children's knowledge, the fish are as follows: perch: p4; parrotfish: p5; bullhead eggs and fry: p6; ray next to an unhatched ray egg: p7; clownfish eggs with larvae inside: p8; pufferfish: p9; swordtail: p10, 11; cichlid: p12; jawfish: p13; stickleback: p14; Siamese fighting fish: p15; discus: p16; arowana: p17; platy: p18; trout: p19; grayling: p20; grunts: p21.